About the Book

As Laura Ingalls leaned back against her seat in the covered wagon, she listened to the lonesome whistle of a far-off train. It seemed to call to her as it went speeding by. "Go on! Go west! Wander and be free!" it cried.

Laura's family is traveling to Minnesota, where they will make a new home on the banks of Plum Creek, near the town of Walnut Grove. Already she has lived in the Big Woods of Wisconsin and the Kansas prairie in Indian Territory, with Ma and Pa and her sisters, Mary and Carrie. But Pa is restless. When he plays his fiddle at night, the haunting music drifts through the house and Laura too feels the wandering spirit.

Millions of children are familiar with the much loved story of Laura Ingalls Wilder from her own cherished "Little House" books and the popular television series, "Little House on the Prairie." Richly textured drawings illustrate the heartwarming story of an independent little girl growing up with determination and pluck, whose travels across the American frontier bring struggle and hard work along with adventure and fun.

A Beginning Biography

LAURA INGALLS
❧ WILDER ❧

by Gwenda Blair

illustrated by Thomas B. Allen

G.P. Putnam's Sons ✒ New York

Text copyright © 1981 by Gwenda Blair.
Illustrations copyright © 1981 by Thomas B. Allen.
All rights reserved. Published simultaneously in Canada
Printed in the United States of America.
Library of Congress Cataloging in Publication Data
Blair, Gwenda.
Laura Ingalls Wilder.
(A Beginning biography)
Summary: A brief biography of the author of the
Little House books which were based on
her own experiences living with her family on
the frontier in the late 19th century.
1. Wilder, Laura Ingalls, 1867–1957—Biography—Juvenile literature.
2. Novelists, American—20th century—Biography—Juvenile literature.
[1. Wilder, Laura Ingalls, 1867–1957. 2. Authors, American]
PS3545.1342Z57 813'.5'2 [B] [92] 79-20758
ISBN 0-399-61139-8
ISBN 0-399-20953-0 pbk.
First paperback edition published in 1983
Seventh Impression
Sixth Impression (pbk.)

To Sasha

The drawings are dedicated in memoriam to Donna Leigh Allen

"Here we are, little half pint of cider half drunk up," Pa said to Laura and stopped the wagon. "Here is where we'll build our house."

Laura and her older sister Mary scrambled down from the covered wagon. They rode in it all the way from their cabin in the Big Woods of Wisconsin to the wide Kansas prairie that was still Indian Territory. Ma always sat straight and quiet in the wagon, but Laura squirmed and fidgeted. It is hard to sit still when there is so much to see and do and hear.

Laura Ingalls was born on February 7, 1867. People in the United States had just finished fighting the long, terrible Civil War with each other. Pioneers looking for better lives were pushing west. Two-and-a-half-year-old Laura was sad to leave the Big Woods in Wisconsin. But Pa said they had to go because all the people moving there were scaring away the wild animals, and the family depended on the animals for food. Besides, he told Laura, she might see a papoose, an Indian baby, in Kansas.

Now Pa built a cabin and a barn with the help of their new neighbor, Mr. Edwards. Laura knew that they had found the right spot, because at night Pa played his fiddle and sang her favorite song:

Oh I am a Gypsy King!
I come and go as I please!
I pull my old nightcap down,
And take the world at my ease!

As she fell asleep, it seemed to Laura that everything, even the moon and stars, was dancing to Pa's music.

Laura and Mary were pioneer girls. Their family was always one of the first to move into a new area.

Their food came from their own fields and the wild animals that Pa hunted. The family made everything by hand. Pa made their house and the furniture too. Ma made all their clothes. She also cooked, washed and cleaned.

Ma taught Laura and Mary to be young ladies. "Wash your hands and faces, girls," she told them every morning when they woke up. Then they put on clean dresses and combed their hair. They helped make breakfast and wash up afterwards. When they went out to play, they wore sunbonnets to protect their skin.

It was a funny thing about those sunbonnets. Mary's always seemed to stay right in place on top of her beautiful golden curls, but Laura's had a way of sliding off her head and down over her long, straight brown hair.

Every day new things happened. Some were fun, like finding birds' nests or wading in the creek, or picking delicious blackberries. But some were scary. When Indians came to call, or wolves and panthers prowled nearby, Laura didn't like it. Pa said the Indians were friendly, but they looked scary to Laura. She was afraid whenever Pa went away on the four-day trip to town for supplies. Once the whole family was so sick that no one could move. They didn't know it, but they had caught malaria from the mosquitoes around the creek.

Christmas that year almost didn't come. The creek flooded and their presents were on the other side. But Mr. Edwards actually swam across with the presents and delivered them. In her stocking Laura found a shiny new tin cup, a stick of candy, a bright new penny, and a heart-shaped little cake that seemed the sweetest thing she had ever eaten. There had never been such a Christmas—never!

When Laura and Mary looked
out from their house, the prairie
seemed flat and empty in every
direction. But the Indians were
still there. They were unhappy
because so many settlers were tak-

ing over the prairie. The next
spring the Indians gathered in a
nearby camp. Every night they
danced and sang and argued about
whether to attack the settlers or
leave.

"I'm afraid of what the Indians might do," Ma said.

"They would be good neighbors if they were treated right," Pa said. "They just don't like being

pushed off their land and getting nothing in return."

Finally the Indians decided to leave the camp. The day they rode away Laura saw a papoose. She

cried because she knew she would never see an Indian baby again.

Soon the Ingalls family left the prairie, too, for the land still belonged to the Indians. By that time, Laura was four, and she and Mary had another sister, named Carrie.

They went back to the Big Woods of Wisconsin for a little while. Mary and Laura went to school with other children for the first time. Then they rode in their covered wagon to Minnesota. It was on that trip that Laura heard her first train. "Go on! Go west! Wander and be free!" it called to her.

When they reached their new home on Plum Creek in Minnesota, they had trouble finding it! That was because it was a sod house, a big room dug into the side of a creek bank. Laura loved the warm creek mud and the whistling rushes, the waterbugs and the little fishes that nibbled her toes when she went wading. Once when she disobeyed Pa and went to the creek alone, a badger tried to bite her. Another time she went swimming by herself and almost drowned. After that she left the creek alone, but it was still hard sometimes to be good.

For Christmas that year the only present Laura and Mary and Carrie got was candy. The family needed their money to buy horses for Pa's wheat crop. Pa was so sure that his crop would be a good one that he built a big new house with lumber that he promised to pay for later.

"A great big girl going on eight should be learning how to read, not running wild along the banks of Plum Creek," Ma said to Laura one day. "You and Mary are going back to school." They lived close enough to the town of Walnut Grove that the girls could walk to school and the family could go to church every Sunday.

Although Laura liked Sunday School, she did not want to go to weekday school. But after the first day, the only thing she didn't like was Nellie Oleson. Nellie called Laura a "country girl" and bragged about being from New York. Somehow it did not make Laura feel better to know that Pa was from New York, too, or that she could throw a ball as well as any child in town.

Then, a week before harvest, a
dark cloud passed in front of the
sun. Millions and millions of
grasshoppers rained down on the

land for days. Ma and Pa tried to
beat them and then to smoke them
out, but the grasshoppers would
not stop eating.

Before the grasshoppers left, they had destroyed Pa's crops and everything else for miles around. There were so many that they squished under Laura's feet when she walked outside. They covered the railroad tracks, and the trains could not move. Worst of all, they laid their eggs everywhere. This meant that next year's crops would also be lost. How could Pa pay for the house and supplies?

"Don't worry," Pa said, and he played his fiddle late into the night. The next day he left to work on other farms far away where the grasshoppers had not come. When he had earned enough money to get the family through the winter, he came home.

That Christmas the church had a party where Laura saw her first Christmas tree. Hanging on it were presents for everyone. Laura was thrilled when the little brown fur cape on the very top of the tree was for her. It was just the right size, and even nicer than the one Nellie Oleson had.

Soon it was 1876, America's centennial, which celebrated the first one hundred years after the country had fought for and won its independence. The telephone had just been invented. For many people it seemed a time of hope. But for Laura's family there was little

good news for a long time to come. The grasshoppers ate all the wheat again, Laura's new baby brother died, and Pa almost got lost in a terrible blizzard.

During the next year they moved six times. Finally they came back to Walnut Grove in Minnesota with a new baby sister named Grace. Soon Pa had saved enough money working in a hotel to build another house. Laura, who was eleven now, had a job too, helping out at the hotel for fifty cents a week.

Then Mary got sick with scarlet fever. She was as patient and as good as ever, but by the time she was better she was blind. Now

Laura had a new task: to be Mary's eyes and tell her how everything looked.

Laura told Mary all about the red velvet seats on the railway car they rode to their next home. Pa was to be bookkeeper at a railroad construction camp in South Dakota. The train went so fast that it was hard for Laura to see the fields and houses that flew by. In just one morning the train went as far as their old wagon could go in a whole week. But still Laura did not believe it when Pa said that someday everyone would travel by train. Someday there would be no covered wagons left.

The land in South Dakota was enormous and still. The settlers had killed all the buffalo, and the Indians were gone. The men who were building the railroad left when winter began, but Laura's family stayed. During the cold winter days Laura and Carrie played outside in the snow, while Mary, who had learned to stitch by feel, sat sewing by the fire. At

night Pa would play his fiddle and sing:

> *I've traveled about a bit in my time*
> *And of troubles I've seen a few*
> *But found it better in every clime*
> *To paddle my own canoe.*
>
> *Then love your neighbor as yourself*
> *As the world you go traveling*
>   *through*
> *And never sit down with a tear or a*
>   *frown*
> *But paddle your own canoe!*

Life was warm and cosy once again.

By springtime the quiet was gone. More settlers were pouring in. Almost overnight the old railroad camp became the crowded town of DeSmet, South Dakota. By summer Pa had built two houses. The one made with lumber left over from the railroad was in town. The other was out on the family's new homestead, where they moved as soon as the ice melted.

Laura had lived in many different towns, but she still liked the country best. "You know how animals will act," she told Carrie, "but you never know about strangers."

The family moved back into town for winter. It was to be the hardest winter anyone in DeSmet had ever seen. For seven months there was a blizzard almost every day. Snow reached the rooftops and no trains could get through with supplies. Laura spent her days twisting hay into logs to burn in the fireplace and grinding the last of their wheat for bread.

In the middle of the long winter, a young man named Almanzo Wilder rode off into the countryside. He came back with a load of wheat that saved the settlers from starving to death.

Christmas that year did not come until May, when the snow melted and the train could get through with presents. After Christmas dinner Pa got out the fiddle that had been silent for so many long, cold months and sang:

Then what is the use of repining,
For where there's a will, there's a
*   way,*
And tomorrow the sun may be
*   shining,*
Although it is cloudy today.

Once again the family moved out to the farm, but life would not be the same as it had been. With the money that Laura earned sewing in town, Mary could go to a college for the blind in Iowa.

There she learned how to read and write in Braille, a special alphabet for blind people. She came home for visits each summer, but they were always too short.

Other things changed, too. Laura and her friends signed each other's autograph books and exchanged fancy calling cards. Laura was studying to be a teacher so she could pay for Mary's college. But more and more often she put down her books to go to a party or a town meeting. At first she felt funny when Almanzo Wilder walked her home on those evenings, but she knew she liked him.

Soon Laura was fifteen and teaching her own school in a town many miles from home. It was lonely being so far away from her family. But Laura knew she had to manage it and she did. Besides, Almanzo brought her home in his sleigh every weekend, even when

the temperature was forty degrees
below zero. Laura loved to ride
beside him in his fast cutter. She
watched the beautiful horses that
Almanzo had trained carry them
back to Ma and Pa and Carrie and
Grace.

Laura grew up as a pioneer girl.

Almanzo was raised to be a farmer. He loved horses more than anything else. Soon Laura was helping him break in a new pair. They rode on the first gravel road built outside of town.

Over the next two years, Laura taught in two more schools. But her teaching days were not to last long. She and Almanzo became engaged to be married, and she would be a farmer's wife.

Pa still called her Half-Pint, but she was eighteen and grown up. Ma helped her make clothes and sheets for her new life. When Almanzo agreed that in the words said aloud in the wedding ceremony, she would not have to

promise to obey him, Laura was ready to be married.

After their August wedding, Laura and Almanzo drove to Ma and Pa's house for a party. Then they went to the house that Almanzo had built for them. Inside were all of Laura's things. After supper that night Laura looked out at the farm and thought of one of Pa's best songs:

Golden years are passing by,
Happy, happy golden years.
Passing on the wings of time,
These happy golden years.
Call them back as they go by,
Sweet their memories are,
Oh, improve them as they fly,
These happy golden years.

The first years that followed were not very golden. Almanzo

and Laura worked hard, but they did not make enough money to pay their bills. Then their lovely house burned down. They had a beautiful daughter named Rose,

but Laura's second baby died. The next year Laura and Almanzo were both very sick, and afterward Almanzo limped for the rest of his life.

Ma and Pa had moved into town to stay. Pa would never go as far west as he wanted, but Laura was determined to go west herself. Finally she and Almanzo drove off in their own covered wagon and ended up settling south in the Ozark Mountains. On a ridge in Missouri they found a little log house and began to make their home there. Over the years they cleared the rocky land and made a good farm. They grew corn, wheat, oats, apples, grapes and strawberries. And they raised hogs, sheep, cows and goats.

Laura and Almanzo's daughter, Rose, went away to high school and became a writer. She traveled all over the world. Laura wrote, too, about farm life for local newspapers. Once she visited Rose in San Francisco. She found it exciting, but she still loved the quiet of the country more than city crowds. By this time Pa's prediction had come true. The covered wagons were all gone, replaced by trains, then cars, and then airplanes.

As the years went by, Laura thought more and more about her childhood long ago. She had been a pioneer girl in the Big Woods of Wisconsin, on the Kansas prairie, at Plum Creek in Minnesota, and in DeSmet, South Dakota. Those times were gone, but Laura wanted to bring them alive again on paper.

In 1930, when she was sixty-three, she wrote her first book. It was called *Little House in the Big Woods*, and everybody who read it liked it. She got so many letters from children asking for more that she kept writing until she had written eight books in all.

"Running through all the stories is a golden thread," Laura said when she had finished. She called that thread courage, independence, cheerfulness and humor. She lived by that thread for ninety years, until her death in 1957. These were the values of those pioneer days of long ago that Laura Ingalls Wilder gave to us.

About the Author

GWENDA BLAIR was born in Washington, D.C. She received her B.A. from the University of Michigan, and did graduate work there, and at the University of California at Berkeley.

She has contributed to many magazines and newspapers, including *Mademoiselle,* the *Village Voice, Reader's Digest, Mother Jones* and *Feature/Crawdaddy.* She was an editor of *Liberation* magazine, and the founder and editor of a news magazine, *Seven Days.*

Currently Ms. Blair is senior editor at *Attenzione,* a monthly magazine for Italians and Italian-Americans, and is working on a film as well.

She lives in New York City with her young son Sasha.

About the Artist

THOMAS B. ALLEN was born in Nashville, Tennessee, where he attended Vanderbilt University. He received his B.F.A. from the Art Institute of Chicago, and has been Chairman of the Department of Visual Communications at Syracuse University. He is an art professor at Southampton College and has also taught at the Parsons School of Design and the School of Visual Arts.

The recipient of the Edward Ryerson Fellowship for Painting, Mr. Allen has also been awarded gold medals by the Art Directors Club of New York and the Society of Illustrators. He has contributed to many magazines, including *The New Yorker, Esquire, Life, Look, New York* and *Sports Illustrated.*

Today he lives in Sag Harbor, New York, with his artist wife Laura. He has three children, Melissa, Ivo and Hilary.

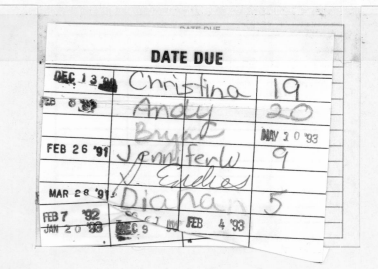